Gain of Function

One hundred and two poems

Gain of Function

Writing No.10

PETER HAGUE

First Published in 2021
by Peter Hague Concept Design Art Direction

ISBN 978-1-8382746-2-7

Cover Design, layout, typography and cover art:
Peter Hague Concept Design Art Direction.

Other photography by Lara Newton.

Also available in hardback: ISBN 978-1-8382746-3-4

A catalogue record for this book
is available from the British Library.

Welcome to this book
and everything I do.
It was never for me –
it was always for you.

Gain of Function

This book represents a shift in creative potential which is exactly described by its title: 'Gain of Function'. You may well have heard of that phrase before, relating to science, and I will explain its specific meaning momentarily. For now though, within the sphere of this book and my work over the years, Gain of Function represents a direct collision between past and future, in which my long-developed ways of working have been suddenly hit by enormous positive change and new possibilities. This change is driven by the advent of social media and also the seismic changes in the world of publishing.

For many years I had toiled at my work, believing that the rigid constraints of the art-world, with its reliance on nepotism, sensationalism and geographic trends would make it impossible for the work I was doing to get a hearing, or be able to breathe itself into something like a beacon-presence, especially since I was not naturally inclined to promote my work in what seemed a stifling atmosphere of unsubtle collusion. I persevered though, hoping my words would add a new voice to the world and also because I felt I had something to say that might be important, or find common agreement.

In fact, I have been writing since the early 1970s and have many creative writings to show for it. With this in mind and with time moving on, I decided a decade ago to devote all my time to pulling my work together and also writing a whole new avalanche of material – much of it poetry. However, the very recent work presented in this book is unique amongst my output, because for the first time I was faced with the possibility that whichever poem I was working on, it could be immediately presented to the public, and indeed to the world via social media. This new reality created a completely different working atmosphere, especially since I was used to working on individual poems for months or even years. The sudden, tense focus of instantaneous publishing added a whole new factor of concentration, necessary confidence and to some degree, embedded topicality, specifically in the poems dealing with the recent virus and some aspects of politics and the media. I was pleased by the way my need to express myself answered this new calling, and also by the natural way the poems seemed to have inherited a crucial devotion to being heard by others. Some of these poems took a relatively short time to write, which seems outrageous to me, given my previous depth of circumspection. However, since they have been under my continual scrutiny for quite a while now, I continue to be pleased with their freshness and accuracy. In fact, bearing in mind that all creative work may somehow be regarded as 'channelled', I believe many of these poems are a sort of perfection and will certainly stand up to 'close reading'.

About a third of the poems in this book were first published on Twitter between 2019-2021 and these dates have been referenced at the bottom of their respective pages. The rest of the poems were written with the similar constraints of urgency and the potentially immediate adrenaline of exposure, even if they were in the end, held back by my own reluctance to release my work, which remains a problem for me. This majority of lingering poems no doubt received more attention than those actually released early and published, but I still wrote them with the vigour of expressing myself to an immediate audience. I hope you enjoy reading them and find them worthy investigations of the many questions and experiences we are faced with today.

The term 'gain-of-function' is more commonly attached to the relatively new research path within the boundaries of epidemiology, also known as gain-of-function research. This controversial branch of potentially unethical exploration into the dangerous world of viruses and epidemics has been the focus of much debate. In fact, in October 2014 a moratorium was announced in America by the National Institute of Health in order to halt such research until it was better understood – a ban which was lifted three years later. In the light of recent developments worldwide it is easy to see why many scientists are concerned. The whole discipline behind this research is that of interfering with lethal pathogens of pandemic potential to increase their virulence and transmissibility, then basically see what happens, hopefully within the confines of a laboratory. Such research is undertaken by scientists from many countries, including China, America and Great Britain. Their attempt at ethical responsibility rests on the suggestion that such research might improve our chances of avoiding or dealing with such pandemics, should they happened to occur naturally in nature.

While the term gain-of-function is an appropriate

concept for this book and my latest poetry in general, I think such work in the field of epidemiology should be resisted again and for good – and although a link between this research and the current epidemic has not yet been established, there are some very interesting coincidences involved.

Some of the poems relate to this controversy and to the virus itself. These are 'Gain of Function', 'Wet-Market to Mall', 'Once in Panic', 'The Quiet Virus' and 'The Death Next Door'.

Other poems that need special comment are 'Death's Duplex', which is dedicated to the American poet, Jericho Brown. It is my attempt to write a poem worthy of his 'Duplex' form, which has a complicated line structure and is based on a mix of forms, from the sonnet to the ghazal and the tonal shifts of blues lyric. I like the natural word play it generates.

Two poems: 'Relocation of the Heart' and 'A Place in the Universal' were both published in 'Poets of 2020', a book produced by Fevers of the Mind Press. Also published by Fevers of the Mind in March 2021 was 'Following Leonard' – a poem dedicated to the memory of Leonard Cohen. 'Dark in the Woods' and 'Eco Warrior – Future as Promised' were published in The Anthropocene Hymnal – an anthology of poems on the theme of climate change and biodiversity loss.

There are also two attempts at Haiku, with its form of three lines containing five, seven and five syllables. These are: 'New Adventures in Haiku' and 'The Six Gifts'.

Peter Hague

About the Author

This book stems from one of the most creative periods in the author's life. A time when he finally decided to commit his remaining existence to writing and to the study of poetry and philosophy. Other artistic considerations were put to one side.

Although Peter Hague has been writing throughout his life, and it was at the forefront of his creativity in the 1970s, it always seemed to take a backseat in the busy world that was his career as a creative director. However, in 2016 at the height of a successful period of working in the medium of digital 3D art, he decided that writing and poetry had always been the potential contact with the public that his visual work lacked. He also thought he was falling short of the depth of artistic contribution he was seeking, so he started writing again. At first he worked through the old material that he had written in the previous decades, but soon had a fresh creative surge and began to write anew, and there are a number of original books in the pipeline to show for it. His current book: 'Gain of Function' is now spearheading this new urgency and the title, when considered overall, literally speaks volumes.

When asked in a recent interview whether he feels he should have stuck with writing more tenaciously through the earlier decades of his life, he said that he felt he had done his writing justice at the various times it had arisen. He said he had always given his writings and poems *the full measure of focus – it's just that I was not very productive at convincing publishers to give it a go – or more likely I genuinely couldn't be bothered with that side of things.* He added that he did not regret being more forward with a marketing strategy and cannot imagine a world in which his writing came out sooner than it did. *"It would have changed things that didn't need changing – lost some things that it didn't justify losing. In some ways, I could be described up to the last five years as being a 'latent poet', but I consider myself a writer of the present and of the future, and if I get the programme through before I die, and also write the new work I have ideas and drafts for, I will be happy. As for the older work, I have kept almost everything I have ever written and many of those poems are already organised into books, because that is how they were first perceived. Even so, I may well produce a 'best of' for the very early work, or combine some volumes."*

Although the initial work seems modern in its core sensibilities, there is certainly some bridging work he needs to complete to bring this work into contact with what he is doing now. He is also working on an anthology in the form of a trilogy that will contain all the new work he has created in the years between 2016 and this 'Gain of Function' anthology. It is telling, with all this in mind, that from the very beginning in 1972, he has always numbered his poetical works and you will notice that this book is counted as writing No.10.

Gain of Function is to be launched almost simultaneously with what he calls his 'bridging book', which is a short, but fascinating construction that connects the future with all that went before it. It is entitled: 'Hope in the Heart of Hatred' and contains some of his own photography as a symbiotic element.

Index of Poems

Bandwagons are Ignorance

Index of Poems continued

Gain of Function

Ageless Games

The sea, my treacherous friend,
has overlapped the sand
in search of incredible dreams.
Rolling those stolen horizons –
back from the perished nightmares
of her drowning souls.

Death fears no death. The sea fears no death.
And cannot bring a caring wave
to launch this brutal hour
of ageless games.

Aspects of Ritual

As these ebbing years roll on,
we must remain in step
with the courage of our words.
Unafraid to reveal the implicit vibration
of their common message.
And although wounded, as we are,
by this lawless comedy of chance and patience,
we must speak without reservation
into the mouth of coming judgement.

Black Message

If this black bone could speak again,
I would take my comforts to the edge of the sea –
let the waves draw me in –
a period of tides
lasting several years.

My loss of you, would be a setting free –
yet my voice would taste of all our memories.

The Churning Sea

The churning sea
calls me –
rolls back a lost time
under wings of living breath
and calls me,
with its spreading tide,
to be free.

I hear the tread of pebbles,
smashed with sand –
as a wave claws back
its free air…
to churn again – with a small liberty,
only the gargantuan oceans understand.

Here, the agreeable waves
stir dawn's evolving glimmer
into millions of years
of monotonous life.

Waving and Drowning

We were neither waving nor drowning,
but now we are both –
happy to slip each current's reach,
down through the back door
that locks our depression.
Deeper we go – to defeat rock bottom,
and wave goodbye
so you will not think badly of us.

Signs of Gods

I am the siren of forgiveness –
chosen by the gods to irritate your ears.
My noise tells you no one matters,
and only men of faith will say otherwise.

The real gods stand behind them,
warming their hands on this pure dissent.
For gods rely on trouble and falsehood
to provide the absolute absolution.

Heaven is rumoured to exist though –
it is said to be here in the miles of your hearts.
Somewhere between prayers of expected devotion
and breath in the grateful deeps of lungs.

The gods spare you this infringement of secular faith,
so long as it remains durable and compliant
with all the misery of tedious life
and the minor disappointments of popular worship.

The Queen of Bees

As she walked the streets, the zealous bees
flew in and out of her extensive pockets.
Some thought it monstrous – others pitied her.
Some thought it tragic – while others blamed magic.

Most people threw coins into an upturned hat
she had glued to her hair, using spoonfuls of honey.
Never once thinking – The Queen of all Bees –
should be scarce of money.

The Abacus

A sliding abacus of human birth.
Each adds their momentary value
to the sum of human worth.

 First published on Twitter – 28 July 2019

Tree

We stayed alive for a long time
after grandparents went first –
stepping back, in entirely expected ways.

Aunts and uncles seized the present.
And only when our parents passed
did these brothers and sisters slide away.

All gone – no one left to rely upon.
Then our elder siblings passed –
in not quite unexpected ways.

And so we are here –
at the beginning of play.
New markers in the long game of death.

Our grandchildren will know the way.

The Distraction of the Soul

Do not punish me for writing poetry –
nor envy its ungoverned spirit with a frown.
It need not claw a path through your heart,
or unsettle your surprise with a compliment.

It hates your ambivalence, but so do you –
this mutually organised failure of the soul.
Try to be a portent of something new –
find a submergence in common intent.

Share a belief in the riches of hindsight.
Otherwise, the world may derail its patience,
skittering its axis a degree off balance –
becoming a more grudging and slanted place.

The Harshest Voice

Disfigurement comes with blood tokens –
the self-harmer's message to all.
The redeemable slash-tag
of frustration and misery –
the wounded call.

The Bridge of Paper Sails

That wayward spirit had no spirit left
when taken down like a sail, from death –
wrapping assuaging arms
around the hindered wings of adjourned flight.

Maybe she wants to be stopped –
but shall we take that careless risk?
The plunge is deep into the heart;
the ground is harder than the fist.

There will come a time
when there is no key behind that final step –
the door to going back will be locked –
the shallows of our tender ship, inept.

Treacherous Minds

He sits in judgement now – on the old step.
Revealing the horrors
shaken loose by vanity's disorder.
He points to a future, but tells us not to visit –
not with jaded boots and treacherous minds.

Our heavy-handed footstep is too dark a shadow –
he warns of the horrors we have all long-feared.
And yet in fear, we do nothing but scorn his guidance
with our deeply flawed version of common sense.

He will soon be moved on by the broken police –
His message being impeccable
and too much to bear.

Held in Transit

The cruelty of the guards
was born of evil boredom.
While we, in pantomime clothes,
were made to feel life's anguish.

It played the keen of our senses
like a Dachau violin.
Exploiting mile-long moments,
that we would in freedom, treasure.

But this was our existence –
this was our measure:

Harassed characterisations
from which we sought no refuge.
Nor did we need haste's conclusion
in the swamp of true bondage.

Eco Warrior: Future as Promised

I was green in nineteen-seventy-two.
I'm not green now and know too much.

There was still time then, but none were listening.
Now there's no time and no one is listening.

Experts talk in terms of warnings,
but only from a standpoint of accepted decimation.

There is no measure of attempted avoidance –
humans expand into one, brutal nation.

Animals and landscapes are labelled 'endangered' –
ushered into the memories of a broken planet.

Yet they continue to star in films and photographs –
a foolish compensation for those who care.

A worrying alternative for the predicted extinct,
said by some – and by those visual gamers –

to be available forever
on a hard drive marked: 'nature'.

Painful Accuracies

1

My library is awash with sad balloons –
I fill them daily but they deflate.
I fill them hourly – they go flat.
I cannot live with their consistent betrayal.
I cannot live with their reliance on pressure –
at either end of any scale.

They keep their extremities a spine away,
balancing their envelopes of impertinent air.
I am left defenceless and gasping for dreams.
My sleep becomes the sleep of the sleep of despair.

Later, I will walk in the park and charge my smile,
then return to write a full inch of words –
fool myself that my mentor was a poet,
while I, a thin-kid writing ice-cream lyrics –
followed-on with dutiful surprise.

2

In the long, fidgeting sounds of night,
the half-asleep, rustle their streets of dreams.
A dark hand unfolds a darker light,
to dim the shores of approaching days.

I will soon connect with these noises of the night –
to their overflow of tantalising sounds.
Some say it's the reluctance of cooling pipes –
some say it's the stark intent of slanted moonlight.

Others say it's the books, all breathing at once –
every book a balloon, with its hiss of deflation;
every book a conclusion of brief salvation,
as each author stiffens their spine
to trouble the world.

Dogs of Any War

War sneaks up on you like a dog.
It won't tell you who wags its tail,
or who calculates the angle of its ears.
It will be financed to include death on all sides.
Later, you will entertain its guest presence
at the solemn remembrance.
It will spit in your eye.

If only we could be free of these demagogues
who stir the controls of high office –
devoid of skill, practice or purpose –
the latest Sonny Jim with an army up his sleeve.
Men without insight – men without eyesight.
They turn up for lunch and dine on your patience –
they farm the discord of your own bitter hatred,
then spit in your eye.

A Place in the Universal

Here, on the bright side of death
I occupy the right side of my heart.
I am at the centre of my being –
a line scribed from head to soul –
a blend of genes, running pole to pole.
I am at the centre of my living dial –
at the confluents of patience, blood and bile,
and all revolving in the universal smile –
that inherent affinity –
Dispensing an axis
for all.

Self Reliance

Come out of the dark; come out of the blue.
There is a road where you don't have to dream
something true.
What you say and what you do
is the new way to stare equality in the face –
to breathe its values –
far beyond a smile of defeat
and discounted sense of place.

Enquiry of the world is all you need
to bring the distances closer to –
bring them forth with blesséd focus;
tune them in, to a valid aspect.

You may see the clouds have a sense of future,
dispersed by sun to bring you through –
to that perfect centre of delivered purpose;
to that place of belonging that begins anew.

The Journey of the Self

Somewhere, is the mortal part.
Elsewhere is the heaven.
Somehow is the road we travel
scouted by the raven.

Message is the truth we bring
in simple verse, or sonnet.
Hopeful is the journey's end.
Happenstance, the ticket.

The Narcissist

I don't like the way your golden sun
is slipping into darkness.
God did not give you
the book of glory –
to see it become a failing majesty
of vain intention.

You have become scattered like weeds
onto a paused opportunity –

Growing without dignity
amongst the egotistical rage
of jealous flowers.

2

Gain of Function

Self Prophecy

We were born looking backwards –
for that was the place of knowledge.
We re-enacted the components of history,
that held examples of a trodden future.
Some futures were labelled prediction,
while guessing had no scent or favour.
All we knew was: we grew like branches –
from the rogue stem
of delinquent behaviour.

The nineteen-fifties
were the measure of intellect.
The nineteen-sixties
were of war and freedom.
But these decades were disciples
of the coming apocalypse,
and its screw is inching
into your future's ear.
It is blowing in the face
of this frowning millennium
and blowing in the wind
when you fail to listen.

A Minor Cancellation

If you have been cancelled recently,
explore the pale new world – your welcome prison.
You will find it no different to the old game of poker,
yet surprisingly, you hold all the cards.

A pair of cancellers
become a conspiracy against freedom –
cancelling themselves out
into a negative entrenchment.

In modesty, you fold your four unseen aces,
while the cancellers weep
into a pair of nothings.

Contradiction Has its Say

Everything contains its own contradiction.
Although I have never witnessed this apparent truth.

Mr Schrödinger's Matinee

The reels go round – the movie plays on,
lighting the darkness in fanciful ways.
The auditorium is still – except for a moth –
a virus has baffled the audience home.
The projectionist died of an unexplained riddle;
a supporting feature he had come to rely on.
Yet the beacon goes on, stating its message –
squinting through the dark and the eyes of the dead.
A film played for a moth, in a system of duty.

Mr Schrödinger walks by in packets of daylight –
an afternoon of sunshine, expanding the hours.
Not knowing if the film is alive or not,
but assumes so, given the time of day.
Without an audience, time has congealed –
it is indeed that time of day, yet not –
not without the irritations of spectator assemblage,
and their drawing of breath in complacent witness.
And not without the projectionist stirring his coffee –
waiting for the reel to outrun the clock.

Time is different without the witness of crowds,
where particles dance in a language of culture.
They make each showing of a film, unique –
as the moth becomes a butterfly, so to speak.

The seat numbers are not specified now,
while unmarked by their brethren, human flag –
or by untested moments in the counting eye
that become meaningless symbols
on the chart of identity.
Like the wavering lustre of a moth's wing –
flapping or not – did it change anything?
Its waves and echoes of awkward flight –
a mere luminance of particles, gathered in light.

Mr Schrödinger leans forward a moment, to listen –
still outside the muse of his broader demonstration.
He reaches with his mind into the absence of being,
imagining the story in celluloid frames.
The liberated audience – all elsewhere –
are fully present in this experiment of cognition –
just as I imagine your company, attached to this poem,
where the ink is informed by your closest reading.
The poem is written in the illumination of trust;
comfortable in the cause of uncertain moments.
It is indeed that moment now, yet not –
and we are all both living and dead, as part of our being.
The energy of the projector and the space between frames
are drawn from the expectant sum of a city's life.
And that, my friend, is the answer to everything.

New Adventures in Haiku

But is this Haiku
or simple word conundrum?
Think for a moment.

 First published on Twitter – 2 February 2020

Twenty Twenty

On New Year's Eve
life offered adventure and reprieve.
On New Year's Day
I saw myself going the other way.

My Dark Peripherals

From the edges of my sight
I see a progression of human visions.
I see them stepping forward
as if to engage my private light.

Yet all these many ages
are unfolded, only briefly,
as they move aside for countless actors,
with their various plays and mysteries.

These seasons – dressed in many styles
of human change and complication –
open their drawers to fill the night,
with mourning minds and forgotten faces.

And so my stage of sight is borrowed
by these woven ghosts of unthreading years.
Treading their vague, yet required performance,
into the various anthems left by others.

The Confusion Birds

On the square lawn
at the mid-morning quiet,
five pigeons pick their way
through the green calm.

Yet sensing a waft
of nervous presence,
in morning's otherwise
stout indifference,

they unfold their wings
in regardless response,
to leave their stage
of complicit symmetry.

And with a prevailing panic
of scattered feathers,
they seem to abandon
everywhere at once.

A Trail of Feathers

Humans hurt humans
and restrict everything else.
Yet cats are licensed
to wander in furtive cycles –
the strides and stops –
the ranging eyes.
The guilty pleasure
of frowned upon blood.

Loved by humans,
they are obliged to linger,
choosing the killing fields
of leaves and lawns.
Stalking communities
of local birds –
plotting their version
of human atrocity.

Trouble is Automatic

Trouble comes – reinventing itself.
Brawling in doorways –
or in anticipated envelopes;

those packets of anxiety,
falling from the mainstream –
a reminding future,
held in delay.

We listen for the sonar,
bleeding from doormats –
an enduring impatience,
pulsing a tedious dread.

Suburban Rainforest

For Lara

Shout out for the showers, weather girl –
let us drizzle with the rain.
Let the clawing wind prevail
and the guzzling drain.

Let the secret web of moss
that lingers in our lawn.
Draw inside its dripping hand
a cherished, greener dawn.

Let the urgent trees we planted,
throughout this, our darkest year,
exhale a mask of better air
and expel all fear.

The Energy of Time

The beach at low tide,
bears the brunt of sunset colours –
falling short of the sad day going,
it turns its ratchet waves of time.
Spectators make no difference
when tomorrow is on its sturdy wing –
already out-guessing the truth and fantasy
in every stolen, little thing.

Death by Statue

For many years I seemed young and lean – like a captain.
Now I am cast as old and foolish – a pitiful general.

Being captain was more fun –
even though I aspired to the status of hero –
even though I can still lay claim
to all the petty factors governing the universe.
I get a salute from every soldier and every nurse.
See them stop and kneel as they go – tying their boots
into the gravity of parade;
gathering up stones to salute my heart,
or to throw at my detested costume –
the flag of my charade.

Nevertheless, we are all comrades here;
on peaceful days, we search for a cause to slap full of anger,
violence being the first response of fearful souls;
Joy is fuelled only by thoughts of furlough –
just as my horse now winters in a foreign field.

My rank is valued only in antiquity,
where the historical insights of pointless battles
are now elevated by irrelevant truths
into the modern skirmishes of minor politics.
A statue comes to stand for nothing
in a nation divided by diverse factions.

Relocation of the Heart

The walls of this unfamiliar house
have transformed themselves
into the closest copy
of where I last felt comfortable.

It is not their fault
that paper peels and paint cracks –
or new feet stroll across the creaking floor.
It is an unburdened wish
to liberate change.

A Sentient Being

If I kill a fly
is it I inside that fly?
Is it really I
who die
if I kill a fly?
Is there a falling sound
as part of me
falls to the ground?

Gain of Function

Death is coming –
its shadow sits on every heart,
as grief leaks its fertile blood,
one grave at a time –

Not too young –
an unsettling euthanasia.
Delivered by obsession,
and a shrinking world.

An insidious revolution,
overwhelming our burdens
with a crushed prosperity
and the silence of peace.

As the first wave rebounds
from the squalor of population,
we wear its shadow
like a stiff, new coat.

The Tower of Twitter

Twitter's babble can be heavy in the rafters of my attic –
a volume almost reaching the notions of Heaven.
Yet seeking parity, rather than sanctity:
a mumbling of crowds talking louder than God –
an endless stream of questioning anxiety.
It is a forum to test all those tenuous beliefs
that the urgent moment then rolls away –
hiding each proposition
behind the stiff swipe of fingers,
though remaining fluid, once caught by the eye.

The Tower of Twitter is a falling presentation
of beacon souls, lighting their world.
You may hear a whisper
drive the algorithm down from the mountains.
Though sometimes you will need a search party
to locate the faintest echo.

A Louder Truth

The tides of Twitter wait for no one,
they roll their wishes to be spun.
Delivered in moments of endangered speech,
randomly garbled into the endless stream.

Tides that wash from the silence of rooms,
pouring words across the face of the deep –
across the curve of our half-eclipsed, elastic globe,
where quiet minds pray for a louder truth.

Soon, there will be nowhere else to look
as space goes quiet, behind thickening clouds.
And we slide our open doors tight shut
to welcome the multi-face of zoom.

Freedom of Thought

We must swim in the depths
of all the brains we have.
Not towards politics or bandwagons –
but for truth.

What little we may find there
will help distil the slow elixir
of vital knowledge.

And of right conduct.

And of love.

Where simple days
and small things matter.

3

Bandwagons are Ignorance

Lives Matter

We are all enslaved now.
A virus owns our lives.
I watch it creep out of sight,
from behind my new procrastinations.
Whole days spent hiding inside
with the windows shut
and the curtains closed.
Yet the dumb TV seems full of crowds,
intent on breathing each other's air.
My mind is sealed by fear.
I hear the pause of the super-spreader –
some poor guy who lives on cigarettes
and blows propaganda in your face.
He won't stop until the virus kills him,
but it won't kill him – he's the slaver's son –
a true captain of cancel and revenge.
He knows the score – He knows the whip.
And has come to bring the world
to its knees.

The Way of Paranoia

If you develop eyes
in the back of your head
they will only serve
to dement your courage.
They will introduce thoughts
that blister and distract –
that follow and question –
reproach and chide.

Set your gaze forward
to binocular distance.
Develop a camouflage
for the sacks of your flanks.
It will deny the suspicion
of psychotic persistence –
deny the endurance
of neurotic scrutinies.

Existence Denied

We're off to the loud sounds –
killing the road with fire.
An oblivion of speech,
using under-words.
Learning that death is an old tale –
a place of fruitless seeds.
We lean back into existence –
not knowing.

Stolen Grief

Buried safe in the night,
like a knife in its sheaf,
we see history alight
on the box of mischief.
It retells the tale
of its journey – its grail,
through the hollow words
of borrowed grief.

Uncommon Sense

Creative people should not be tempted
onto the delicate scales of ill-balanced doctrine.
Once seen to be one-eyed –
blind to some uncomfortable truth,
they are quickly discounted –
pushed beyond the purity of credible air.

Do not deny your truth its full measure –
we have almost all the same features;
almost all the same flaws.
The thin, stretched canvas that supports our talent
must not be strained by a ripple of deceit.

Subjective notions are amongst those things
we should never truly profess to know.
We should go forward into the glow of truth,
as politics step backward onto a page of uncertainty –
and into the unreliable duplications
of a modified past.

Presented News

Blood drips from their spritely mouths
as they change the public's mind
on the last official word.

The Conspiracy of Edited News

Good morning, I see the television is on.
Has anything changed?
Or is it truth, told wrong?

The Undermining Editor

And there is marching in the street
as humankind discover the worst things to do,
then do them with spite – do it complete.
Pouring poison on an invented weed –
presenting a broken world, ripe for healing,
but with the suggested medicine of anger and denial.

Yet to err is human – and so shall it be:
speech unbridled – insults for discussion.
We need to know what people believe –
there are no solutions in practical concussion.

The media urge the protest on,
then go quietly straight, in confirmed contradiction:
each reporter nailing privilege to the wind –
while sniping words at the flags of commonality.

These parasites are esteemed in unquestionable honour –
and in the comfortable hug of team reporting.
It has nothing to do with balance or journalism –
just a wink to the editor's insidious page:

"You did your best, comrades – and so did I.
We made freedom of speech
sound like surrender.
We made freedom of thought
a slanted sigh."

Stars, Stripes and Union Jacks

I command by doing nothing.
I lead by example.
Things are going badly,
but in an orderly manner.

The first to disobey orders
may take up the dubious mantle –
that of all-encompassing leader –
the commander of nothing.

It is worth a better uniform –
dry-cleaned every evening,
but I will stand-down graciously,
should candidates have my measure.

I am too young to waste my time
pretending leadership of anything –
of any form of movement –
any army of nothing.

The Candle

Written from a photo-prompt: a candle flame

The candle's light reveals all
when it strikes the nearest wall.
But when it strikes the closest face
a deeper shadow takes its place.
A deeper dark, lit by shapes –
the flickering expressions
emotion makes.

Agreeable Visions

The look of love
has never been constrained
by the judgments
of worthiness or beauty.

Hair Without Words

Written from a word-prompt: 'Ulotrichous'

She had beautiful hair –
a storm of curls.
It did not need an ugly name.
No audible word – no scripted lust –
no need for lips to lose their trust.

The silence of sin palabras will do?
I will ignore 'Ulotrichous'
and so should you.

Back Word

Advance on the spring of palindromes –
elasticated duality in the making.

Speak no ill, dear friend,
lest your maladies sink into the merging lies

between the two fine peaks of tenet health,
or the collapsed bookends of forgotten knowledge.

Life is wounded between these rising peaks,
where maladies sink into the valley of lies.

Speak not, dear friend, of this elasticated unmaking
and advance on the spring of palindromes.

Remembrance Sunday

For Winifred

A service to take part in –
remembering the war
her father served in.

Friend and Foe: The Next Suspicion

Foreigners are dangerous to each other
and all of us are foreigners on this Earth.
My neighbours are friendly foreigners –
yet unpleasantly English, like me.

We're dangerous people, even to ourselves.
We are cruel, especially to each other,
and we are also great friends of the breathing universe,
and all the singing languages that separate our song.

Yet even now, as I prepare to wither –
to die at the hands of a foreigner or a friend?
I will choose a foreigner quite likely to be jolly,
and were it not for the war, quite a jolly good friend.

An accepted acquaintance among these rumours of war,
yet already spied on – as the friend of the enemy.

Should We Be Ordinary Folk

A poem is a distracting daydream –
we gaze behind the poet's lucid stare.
Yet, should we be ordinary folk, and this be winter,
we could engage ourselves with tending fires –
the ever-ebbing cycle, that takes
our seasoned comfort prisoner –
that leaves the sins of extraordinary guilt
to cool in the moribund ash of a petrified hearth.

We poke through the carbon dust
of this wounded oracle –
still looking for signs in the delicate wreckage –
the charred remains of our ancestors' minds –
affording the credulity of kings and queens.
Yet encouraging words to be common in their flight,
and in the chapters that exalt our living blood.
Should we indeed, be ordinary folk.

The Broken Seal

The cafe, the company, the coffee.
The cretinous, the clumsy, the cure.
Life is difficult, and often one-worded,
and wonderfully insecure.

The faceless, the famous, the fiction.
The curious, the crumbling, the crumb.
Life has these numerous stations of pity.
And seems always to be overcome.

Drifter

Written from a picture of early snow in Colorado

Even the snow goes
where it normally refuses –
bending foliage before the autumn equinox.
A cold chill settled in the heart of Colorado
after heading south
from nowhere.

Wandering Where Sand Follows

You with the sad face,
amongst the seaside stalls –
the cheerful clatter of sound and colour.
The happy child with vicious parents –
a slap, nerve-ending the whole town.

The eternal wandering
of recounted experience,
finding patterns of place
in spliced decades.
A map of existence
trodden by miles of families,
walking unfamiliar shoes
full of sand and curse.

There is pity in these moments,
accompanied by music –
its loyalty now played
in the yearnings of a foreign air.
As we tread the path
of gifts and amusements.
Searching for the smallest things
that make us care.

Kicking Back Time

A boot of wind splits the meadow –
parting flowers – kicking back time.
We smell the earth of ancient hours,
while telling truths to avoid going home.
We talked in sunshine and laughed in rain –
we had the compass of youth and dreams.
Our stream was the ripple of life and breath,
patrolled by honesty in the deepest realms.

Bandwagons are Ignorance

The clamour of the bandwagon –
its banners and its burning flags,
is soon to fail – on tired ears.
Its confrontation drives the wedge
that sends the party home.

It wallows in a threatened peace
within disowned, disabled minds,
where frustration, time and fake tv,
hold us hostage to false belief.

But we are permanent individuals here,
not needing to weep on gathered shoulders –
the world won't spin our barren way
because we slide on the blood
of expedient injustice.

It won't listen, beyond that first wave
of blind, hollow ignorance –
where the loudest unskilled voice
chimes only for the bitter crumb
of redundant apology.

4

Slapped by Nietzsche

Red Moon

The guards van is gone –
redundant these days
in the sparse remapping
of our current world –

the guard sipping tea
on the end of a train
with trees going by
in skeletal piles –

that vanguard is gone;
that rose lamp is dead –
tobacco extinguished;
a Bible part-read.

A light with no end
shines out of existence –
no valid history;
as dumb as paint –

and the trailing wagon,
with its secular light,
is drawn clear of demons
and the chill of night.

Waiting for the Next Bad Train

How did we get here, anyway –
by catching a spoonful of bad luck?
That's how the blues would have it.

The blues will flag you down at any crossroads –
symbolising freedom, yet confounding inequality.
You may hitch a ride on a six-eight stumble –
unsettling steps toward the shutters of midnight.

It's a damn good rhythm though –
something that moves in time – pulling like a tow –
and perfectly slow.
Lurching forward like a torment –
leaning backbeat into rock.
Four-four time might even tap your foot –
yet discreetly, like you almost forgot…

No doubt waiting for the next bad train
to play those stiff, old rails like strings –
a rhythm caught by fingernails,
as the hollow riff goes sliding by.

A sleeping dog
wakes one eye.

A Carriage Window

Do not alight here, Agnes Brown
for this is not your station.
All the trains now going home
stand rusted in stagnation.

Do not leave your street of steel,
the porter lost your label –
but luggage weighs a journey down
and makes the nerves unstable.

Do not wait here, Agnes Brown,
yon countless sleepers beckon.
Bind their tracks to homeward bound
until your path is woven.

Made of Sky

Tell me on the air,
tell me on the wing –
the voice of true despair
has silenced everything.

My heart is made of mud,
my truth is made of lies.
I wander in the vanity
of boredom and surprise.

So drink before you go –
another day is spent.
The TV passes time.
The sunset pays the rent.

    First published on Twitter – 2 February 2020

Midnight Squall

In memory of Anne Sexton

Here at death's doorway –
gothic and brooding.
Depression is king –
I can't be happy with anything.
Anyone.
Any burst of Sun.
I have checked my sextant
and I am rowing home.
I have done my hitch!
I have crossed my canvas –
stitch by stitch.

Slapped by Nietzsche

I'm pulling out.
I'm giving up.
I am tired of revisiting my coffee-cup.
I gave it all –
I brought my best.
I am far too long into this lifetime quest.
The words were there,
the thoughts were mine –
they took me dancing all the time.
But now I'm tired –
I've lost my thread.
I suppose I said what I wanted said.
I sit alone
in a dying chair.
My Will to Power
no longer here.
My broken bones
refuse repair.
My special looks –
contrived by entropy.

Disfiguring the War

My nurse took off her underwear
and threw it in my face.
I said: "That's no way to treat a veteran –
a veteran and an ace."

She said: "Look, you're only wounded,
but you were wounded in the face
and underwear was all I had
to dress a minor case.

Besides, I came to love you,
not to heal your wounded looks,
but I could never love a veteran
who brags so loud, it sucks.

O I'm glad I came to love you,
not to heal your broken face.
But I cannot love a veteran
who brags he was an ace."

I said: "I was lauded as a hero,
now I'm wounded in my pride.
I'll take my loyal servitude
and join the other side."

An Unbearable Oneness of Being

A pond is a soup of living things –
each eyeball attached to what it sees
by a physical envelopment
of viscous fluid.

It is a living thing,
a world made frightening
by a sense of creatures.
Each bound in irritation
and in the far-flung vectors
of tiny shimmerings.

Eating becomes a habit of survival
beyond the meagre testimony of living food.
We kill to exist, hiding our rivals
in the unjust bag of our swollen bodies –
and in the revolting energy of naked persistence.

We pray for our innocence of the macabre,
yet leave our ripples to tell the tale –
to telegraph a radiating crime of death –
from a warning heart that beats no breath,
except in the wasted bubbles
of a gurgled truth.

Death's Duplex

Dedicated to Jericho Brown: inventor of this form

I don't wanna die, but I feel compelled.
I am guided to the door where death is exhaled.

I'm standing at the door where death is inhaled.
Death is essential to my life, but I close the door.

The door is opened by the pressure I feel.
I live in contradiction of peace and pressure.

My own contradiction is these thoughts of peace.
They draw me aside to make me an offer.

I offer my life to the contradiction of death.
There's a smile on my face and I don't wanna live.

I don't want to die with a smile on my face.
I offer a smile to the contradiction of death.

Death smiles back and seems like a friend.
I feel compelled, but don't wanna die.

The Privacy of Death

In the private light of death
the world no longer owns your image.
Your being is detached
from that awful delusion –

and in the seclusion of that urging dark
your DNA creates an arc –
merging profound details of contraband code
with the electrifying conditions
for auspicious life –

they summon the laws of Lazarus
to an unsealed tomb
and cut the strings of death
with a facial bloom.

Utopia is Difficult

Where will I live when I die?
And what will I do
without my work –
and all the bullshit I now curse,
but will miss like lavish toys,
when I am bored in paradise?

The Beguiling Charms of the Post-virus Revolution

When the left-wing become the right-wing
they will kill the Royal Family.
And you will be glad.
Then they will kill some of your own family,
and your friends
and you will pretend to be glad
or you will be murdered with them.

When the Left change hands
they will open all the doors you were too wary to open –
or too polite to open –
or suddenly too black or too white to open.
And according to your new section leader:
many doors will swing your way
though many more will close behind.

This is the slicing of the cake:
when the post-virus revolution
becomes a left-handed fascist state –
an obsession to begin everything again
with implicit laws, born of revenge –
lending your vote to the faceless idea
of counting overwhelming heads.

They start with ground zero
to explain their intrusion
into what you thought was the better idea of your life –
denying the individuality of your brave persistence,
and your reasonable attempts at personal freedom.

Freedom is never offered by the Left –
they demand only the blind conformity of Utopia.
They will lean their stance to the Right, to nail you,
demanding your identity for their nameless calling –
an exploitable victim, dead or blank.

And they will kill me with their virus
for writing this poem. All future poems
will be commissioned by the state.
And from voiceless poets –
those laureates and loud mouths,
living in the media cocoon
of self-isolation and enveloping terror.

Funeral Song

In the black goodnight
we stir the dark
with all the emotions
of our inner light.

Our time is gone.
We need not fret.
The dead
will guide us
home.

Evening Prayers at Sunset

He rowed towards the Sun, but never caught it –
sometimes it slid behind his noble darkness.

He faced his fears and chased its golden story –
only to feel a furnace rise behind him.

There was no compass then,
only the incomprehension of baffled men –

who spread their compensation of simple worship
into the fluid seed of our yielding days.

The Smile Virus

All the driven bones of Earth
rely upon a moment's mirth.
Where half a smile
might light a day –
release an optimistic force.

Where all our souls are set full-sail
and all our kinder thoughts prevail.
Where negativity is set aside
in the incomparable joy
of a safe exhale.

The Long Fade Into Light

In memory of my parents

Where are you going, Marilyn?
Our eyes have not seen enough.
Your kind of fame demands an encore –
where the trick of eternal youth
is to be painted in clouds.

People are going –
yet our memories retain them,
as they slide into the long fade
of personal loss.

There at the deathbed
of my own Father.
I am always present,
one way or another.

And also that day
in the bright hills of Derbyshire,
where he walked in the warm wind
of eternal youth.
And where he thought he saw Betty,
with hair like Marilyn –
address undisclosed
among painted clouds.

The Captain of a Heart

I am too tired to stand to your attention –
too smothered with unfamiliar navigation to comply.
But since you left this house through the broken door
I have breathed nothing but this sigh.

I have no momentum since you went away –
a broken heart insists only one person stay.
And I am bound in the eternal pity of divorce
and the long salute of this final day.

A Silence

The hours we spent together
and what we meant to each other
are irrelevant now –
they mean nothing.

We were young then,
we were lovers,
and that was our reason –
never to be old.

Never to be two sides
of the same worn out room,
with no excitement
in our square hearts.

Our petrol was youth.
Our reason was love –
now we have neither.
We mean nothing.

State of Play

What is happening to us?
Each day breaks apart
like a fortune cookie –
but without romance or prediction.

There is no – robust – anymore.
All the bolts of engineering
have squirmed themselves loose.
All the chains of industry
have buckled into piles –

the masks we wear exclude our smiles
and the end seems only an inch away –
Or closer
in these stilted metrics.

The Quiet Virus

Written from an anecdote told by my sister

Shopping and weeping
among rumours of virus –
her only son gone –
taken by mystery.
No one in the village
knew anyone
so death was ignored
and will be again.
It will call tonight
for a mother's fate –
the insupposable mystery
of a lost child.
She too will go shopping then,
bereaved by expedience.
She too will weep silence
into rumours of virus.

No One is Nourished

Parasites show the way
to all available systems of self-defeat –
having rinsed the tribe
of everything worthwhile –
whittling it down to branded folly:

Beer clichés and energy drinks
would be an example –
a possession of style, well beyond thirst.

And now the world's mouth
is in your pocket,
asking to be swiped by slick fingers –
the trite possibilities of stylised talk,
blending the communication of a simple smile
into the erratic details of emoticon.

It's like having chewing-gum
stuck to your shoe –
a hanger-on from the old days of stolen adolescence –
a fashionable ploy pretending to be cool,
and yet awkwardly malnourished
and misunderstood.

But no one is nourished –
everyone is chewing –
everyone is sated –
everyone sick of it.

5

The Last Day

The Death Next Door

Did you feel the virus knock,
but only when it knocked next door?
Your own frontier, you can ignore,
but not the knock that knocks next door.

A change of neighbour wakes you up.
You drink a mind-filled coffee cup
and watch the coffin, walked away –
and yet this death, this loss,
this missing soul
is telegraphed as here to stay.

Did you hear the knock next door,
the knock you never heard before?

The Bell

The bell, the bell
the word, the horn.
The hill, the sky,
the earth, the dawn.

The lost, the found,
the weak, the well.
The endless death –
the bell, the bell.

Sleight of Hand

If you are God – or King, under God?
It is your duty of care
to recognise and smite the coming chaos.
You do not have the right,
under the law of thrones,
to appear reckless and ignorant
and point elsewhere.

Enemy Within

The deep ship rolls home,
its bowels carrying an ocean.
A cargo of waves
captured in folly –
balanced in the bilge
between bulkhead and freedom.
They will have this ship sunk
in the coming storm.

Wet Market to Mall

Blind witch, sated muse –
hung in the galleries of the desperately poor.
Potions abound and sordid spells,
each rendered void of attention's scan.
Wool of bat pulled over eyes –
tongue of ferret in disguise.
Did you report a poisoned world,
or just the snake that choked its science?
We are now subsidiary to the blush of expedience,
concealed in the blind-breath of patient masks.
Except for the whispers of blatant truth
that we glimpse in the deep honesty
of magnifying glass –
those silenced shop windows
that mirror our loss
in a stoic gospel of sincere vacancy.

The Journalist's Smile

"Let it fail. Roll it out and let it fail."
No culture can survive
feeding on its own entrails.
It wins, only to succeed
in wounding the palette of future air.

The media transfusion of poison blood
will congeal sharply and say:
"Your vaccine has failed. Go back to the lab."
We have adjusted our smile for the latest news.
Our smile now incorporates a smirk of truth:
and as we say in the headlines: "We told you so!
And now there's proof."

So hail the retreat into the gambled extermination
and the sordid underpinning of a herd-immunity.
"We will continue to support that convenient sacrifice,
and the attempted glory of false progress."
It flavours the world with a positive intervention,
while our best smile and your vaccine
have failed common trust.

Once in Panic

Don't die of Christmas.
Don't die of Ignorance.
You cannot measure death
in missed holidays.

The Six Gifts

Haiku written from a word-prompt: 'box'

A box should open
all its sides, like a puzzle,
returning full value.

          First published on Twitter – 26 December 2020

Hiding the Obscure in the Dark Time of Covid

If I were Thomas Hardy
my poems would attract thousands of likes –
the endorsement of fame is its own glue –
even among the anonymities of human awareness.

As Jude the Obscure I attract a precious, few likes –
yet no doubt genuine and properly considered.
These are gratefully gathered
from the harvest of acquaintance –
a brief harmony
glowing in the willing vibrations of twitter air.

Both anonymities make me strive for recognition.
But only for these poems I am entrusted with.
I don't want them to die alone in a famous pandemic,
gasping for breath, like me.

The Journey to Opus Z

The full gloom of the sea.
The full dark in me.
I will walk into that blizzard of salt –
and set myself free.

Following Leonard

In memory of Leonard Cohen

This could be the darkness
written in your soul.
An elemental darkness,
without the element of control.
It's been murder in the city –
there's plague now, at the beach.
The only goal we truly have
disappoints the reach.

But there's a crazy road to nowhere,
that branches from your heart.
And it's a long, long way to get there –
better make a start.

Raison d'être

If I outlive my two loves
I will die three times.

Every Step Must Be Trodden Once

As this year caves in to the burden of folly,
a new year hosts the responsibility
of noble passage –
but there will be no sanctuary
from this current turmoil – no mercy,
in a dishonest turning of the page.

Life is ultimately sad,
as one important thing passes on –
one driven soul to the next,
all pledging unity.
And it would be better to bleed
than to remain impure –
better to die a sweet old man
with everything said,
than to bear the agreeable scrutiny
of eternal wisdom.

Let us take the beginning and end of our lives
and pull them apart like a Christmas cracker –
endure the baffled conclusion of mirrored eyes,
wearing the eager folly of a paper hat.

The Fullness of Entropy

Everything hurts,
in time.
Sometimes twice.

Blue Awakening

Gonna pray these flowers turn blue
and only come out at night.
Night-people need flowers too
and blue after midnight feels right.

The Last Day

A molten sun saluted into a sundown sea,
folding bitter ships into sweeter waves.
Washing its hands in a darkness of light –
reddening to purple in blackcurrant caves.

And as the gulls and guillemots took flight
and the pools were rendered smooth as balm,
each starfish lived in its own little light
and made a comfort of the calm.

Methods of Reaching You

Desktop – several poems at once –
fragments – usual suspects:
unfinished ideas fermenting overnight.
Quick ones swimming through –
old ones, beached for years.
The aloof, awaiting another reading…
a turmoil of subtle bleeding.
One day, they will pass you in the street, and say…

Dark in the Woods

It will be dark in the woods
when we re-enter its living space
after millenniums of streets
have fallen and failed.
When all we have left
is our lanterns and memories –
and the courage to listen
ourselves to sleep.

When we live amongst trees
we will grow the next stem,
we will unfold a new leaf
to replace our past.
We will learn to share
the simple devices
of art and philosophy,
where the darkness is healed.

There is a Lord of Souls
in the comforting woods
and we will come to know
the benefits of autumn –
when our souls have ceased
their civil reliance –
when all we have left
are lanterns and darkness.

Song of an Empty Earth

When humankind are gone
and the gaping wounds of Earth are healed.
The Earth will say, so long…
So long
So long
So long…

The Empty Hours

You will miss me at 3.00am
when I no longer share
that deepest hour –
when you are alone
in what seemed a comfortable eternity,
but is now only a place called night.

You will miss your remote companion,
and that dark, yet bewitching era –
where he claimed to know the compass of space
and the space within every stillness –

where he frequently questioned
the stubborn quiet
that stalls the leading-edge
of unspoken words –

where the bell of the universe
surrounded all silence,
yet our night was never far from ringing.

I made cuttings from these prevarications
and grew them on, in the simmering minutes.
A propagation blooming in the ripples of peace,
that served the darkness
with a comforting twilight.

It has never once diminished.

So when I have ceased to breathe
into that same shape
where you now find yourself
surprisingly hesitant –

where I have left these hours
to your fond persistence –

where I have withdrawn my pageant
into God's trust –

I will call again
through the binding connections,
where our hearts fused
in a miracle of dust.

Gain of Function
One hundred and two poems